IMAGES
of America

BLACK HAWK AND CENTRAL CITY

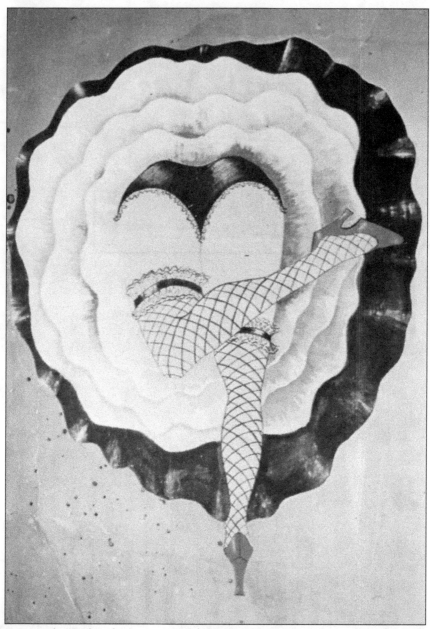

The Fanny on the Ceiling began as a prank but quickly became the trademark of the Glory Hole, a popular Central City tavern that opened in 1946. The painting of owner Emmy Wilson's fanny was based on a stunt from New Year's Eve in 1949, in which she dangled her legs through a hole in the ceiling. The Gilpin Historical Society adopted it as its logo in 2010. (Courtesy of David Forsyth.)

ON THE COVER: A group of miners poses around 1900 near the Little Pittsburg Mine outside of Nevadaville. Gold mining made Black Hawk and Central City world-renowned mining camps and gave them the nickname "the Richest Square Mile on Earth." But, at the time of this photograph, mining was beginning to die out, forcing residents to find new ways to survive. (Courtesy of Gilpin Historical Society.)

IMAGES
of America

BLACK HAWK AND CENTRAL CITY

David Forsyth

ARCADIA
PUBLISHING

Published by Arcadia Publishing
Charleston, South Carolina

Library of Congress Control Number: 2013946707

For all general information, please contact Arcadia Publishing:
Telephone 843-853-2070
Fax 843-853-0044
E-mail sales@arcadiapublishing.com
For customer service and orders:
Toll-Free 1-888-313-2665

Visit us on the Internet at www.arcadiapublishing.com

CONTENTS

ACKNOWLEDGMENTS

Special thanks goes to Alan and Maggie Demers, Alan Granruth, Jim Prochaska, the Forsyth family, Mayor Ron Engels of Central City, Viola Hall Steckel, Ed Lewandowski and the crew at the Hidee Mine, Michel Tritt, Gina Quackenbush, the late Bill Axton, Joyce Axton Jamison, the late "Chocolate" Dan Monroe, Mike Keeler, Jim Johnson, John Moriarty, Dirty Jeff, Spike, and Stacia Bannerman at Arcadia Publishing.

Unless otherwise noted in individual captions, the images in this book appear courtesy of the Gilpin Historical Society.

INTRODUCTION

The Wild West so often portrayed in movies and on television would have seemed very strange to the first residents of Black Hawk and Central City. From the moment miners first arrived in the mountain towns west of Denver, they worked hard to first establish, and then maintain, law and order. The men quickly brought in their families, elected sheriffs, founded churches and schools, built theaters and stores, and joined fraternal organizations (nearly every group, from the Masons to the Elks to the Knights of Pythias, had lodges), all activities that told the outside world that Gilpin County was a stable and good place to do business.

John Gregory discovered the first lode gold deposit in what would become Gilpin County in May 1859, triggering Colorado's gold rush. Within weeks, tens of thousands of men had rushed to the gulch that became known as Gregory Diggings to seek their fortunes. The gulch was then part of the Kansas Territory, but federal, state, and territorial authorities did not have the resources to enforce rules so far west of civilization. As a result, one of the first things the new settlers did was hold mass meetings in order to establish mining districts. Each district had its own rules for staking and recording claims as well as proceedings to deal with lawbreakers that ranged from claim jumpers to murderers. With the establishment of the Colorado Territory in 1861, the mining districts gave way to cities. The city of Black Hawk, situated at the lower end of the gulch, was originally known as Black Hawk Point when the first post office opened there in 1862. The town was named after the foundry in Rock Island, Illinois, that made one of the first stamp mills that came into the area. One mile up the gulch was Central City, which became the seat of Gilpin County. Sources disagree on whether Central City received its name because of its central location in the mining area or for a store that was located there. The two towns quickly became enormously powerful in Colorado, both politically and economically.

Known since 1859 as "the Little Kingdom of Gilpin," "the Richest Square Mile on Earth," or "the Cradle of Colorado," Gilpin County was the smallest county in Colorado until the creation of Broomfield County in 2001. It was named for William Gilpin, the first territorial governor of Colorado, and was one of 17 original counties. County borders were drawn inversely based on population; Gilpin was the most populous and so became the smallest county. But, what it lacked in size, it made up for in many other ways.

In the political arena, Black Hawk and Central City could claim three US senators—Henry Teller, Jerome Chaffee, and Nathaniel Hill—and Colorado's first representative to Congress, Judge James Belford, who happened to be one of the most-respected mining lawyers in Colorado and wrote many of the laws that still govern the mining industry to this day. Teller was also the first Coloradan appointed to a cabinet post, serving as secretary of the interior under Pres. Chester A. Arthur from 1882 to 1885, and Gilpin County's only presidential candidate (though his short-lived 1896 candidacy was initiated without his blessing). A number of other men and women that were influential on the state as well as the local level, including Eben Smith, Bela S. Buell, Horace Hale, and Dr. Florence Sabin, got started in Black Hawk and Central City.

Black Hawk and Central City were just as powerful economically as they were politically. Miners pulled more than 4.7 million ounces of gold from mines in the area, guaranteeing that the rest of the territory (and world, for that matter) would take notice. The founders of Central City's banking houses went on to establish banks in Denver that would play major roles in the state for years to come, such as the First National Bank of Denver, which was cofounded by Eben Smith, Jerome Chaffee, and several other partners. That bank in turn brought David Moffat, who would play a major role in the mining and railroad industry in Colorado, to prominence. The county's mines were so impressive and productive, and its citizens so politically connected, that Ulysses S. Grant visited the area three times (Jerome Chaffee's daughter also happened to be married to one of Grant's sons).

Black Hawk and Central City were at the peak of their power in the 1860s and early 1870s, but Colorado's mining industry began moving on to other parts of the state from the late 1870s to the 1890s. As a result, Black Hawk and Central City saw their star slip just a bit. Even the famous Central City Opera House fell on hard times as Horace Tabor's Tabor Grand Opera House in Denver stole the show and became one of the preeminent theaters in the state. By the early 1900s, gold mining in Gilpin County was becoming less and less profitable, but the residents of the two towns persevered and continued with life as they knew it.

World War I brought a temporary halt to the mining business in Black Hawk and Central City, which in turn brought economic decline to the towns long before the Depression of the 1930s wreaked havoc on the country's economy. People left the towns in droves, sometimes with only what they could carry in a suitcase or trunk. A brief mining revival in the 1920s looked promising for Gilpin County, but it soon fizzled out, and World War II forced the mines to close once again. Miners expected to reopen the mines as soon as the war was over, so many simply stored their equipment inside the mines and locked them up. Unfortunately, most of them were never reopened.

But, the towns were far from dead. Residents of Black Hawk and Central City found themselves in a new boom period as tourism, driven in part by the reopening of the Central City Opera House in 1932, became the dominant industry. People from all over the world were eager to visit authentic American mining towns, and few were more authentic than the two small towns in Colorado's mountains. They were so authentic, in fact, that the Central City/Black Hawk Historic District was declared a National Historic Landmark in 1961. When tourism began to dry up in the late 1980s, Black Hawk and Central City (and Cripple Creek, 140 miles to the south) turned to legalized gambling. A new boom period resulted, and once again, the two towns survived. Through boom and bust, this is their story.

One

MINING GOLD
1859–1873

In the fall of 1858, John H. Gregory, an experienced miner from Georgia, left his wife and five children behind as he set out for the gold fields of British Columbia. A brief stint as a supply-wagon driver led him to Fort Laramie, where he heard of gold discoveries on Cherry Creek and the South Platte in what would eventually become the Colorado Territory. Intrigued, Gregory abandoned his mission to Canada in order to prospect in the Rocky Mountains. He was certain he had found gold in what is present-day Black Hawk in April 1859, but a heavy snowstorm forced him to abandon the site until May, when he returned with eight other men. On May 6, 1859, Gregory located and staked two claims on what would soon be known as the Gregory Lode. He described the initial find, saying that although snow and ice prevented the men from digging too deeply, the first pan of surface dirt gave up $4 in gold; over the next two weeks, he earned $972 from his claims before selling them for $21,000 and going to work prospecting for other miners at $200 a day. Within a few weeks, more than 3,000 men were at work in Gregory Diggings; by July 1859, that number had swelled to between 20,000 and 30,000 people. According to Denver's *Rocky Mountain News*, living conditions in the mining camp were at first primitive, with people huddled in tents, wagons, log cabins, dugouts, and houses made of any readily available material. Residents were eager to let the world know that theirs were permanent mining camps, however, and worked hard to settle the mining districts and keep them law-abiding places with families, sheriffs, and strict laws. The first appearance of the name *Central City* was in November 1859, and use of the name *Black Hawk* followed that spring. Other mining camps in the area included Mountain City, Dog Town, Russell Gulch, Nevadaville, and Bortonsburg. Some of these other camps lasted only weeks, while others survive today, but they all had one common reason for their existence: gold.

John Gregory, who discovered lode gold on May 6, 1859, between Central City and Black Hawk, is seen here in the only known photograph of him. Gregory Diggings eventually became part of Mountain City, which in turn became part of Central City. Based on business directories, he moved in and out of Colorado until at least 1876; his ultimate fate, however, remains a mystery.

The first miners in Central City and Black Hawk engaged in placer mining, more commonly known as panning for gold. An experienced miner could process 50 pans a day but had to recover at least one ounce of gold from those 50 pans to turn a profit. This image of men engaged in placer mining near Central City in 1859 is one of the first photographs ever taken in Colorado.

PLACER MINING IN EARLY DAYS

This picture, taken near Cripple Creek in 1894, shows the tents that the first miners in Black Hawk and Central City called home. Commonly known as pyramid or range tents, they provided sturdy shelter for the men seeking gold. Judging by the "Keep Off The Grass" sign to the left of their tent, the Rinker brothers, seen here, were a humorous pair.

Placer deposits were created by water washing gold from underground deposits into creeks and rivers, and they were quickly depleted, making placer mining a short-lived business. This forced miners to search for rock formations that indicated the presence of lode gold, the source of the placer deposits. That is what these two men are doing near Central City in the early 1900s.

This is the earliest known photograph of Central City, taken in about 1860. The tents of the early prospectors had quickly given way to log-cabin homes and stores. The town was rapidly turning into a thriving community, and by the time this picture was taken, it had an assayer's office, theater, bank, and several supply stores. According to one report, by August 1859, there were already 300 buildings in town. One early visitor to Central City marveled at the way tents and cabins in the town seemed to defy gravity and cling to the sides of hills and mountains. (Courtesy of Denver Public Library Western History Collection, X-63199.)

Looking down Lawrence Street in Central City toward Black Hawk in the early 1860s, the assay office in Graham's Drugstore is prominent in this picture. Assayers were considered royalty in mining camps because their reports could make or break a mine. Through a complicated process, assayers determined just how much gold was in a ton of ore produced by a mine. Some mining companies even had their own assayer in order to guarantee the results of such tests. One of the longest-lasting assay offices in the county was J.S. Kimball's, built next door to the Teller House in the 1870s. (Courtesy of Denver Public Library Western History Collection, X-2658.)

Black Hawk had also grown into a thriving community when this picture was taken in the mid-1860s (the Presbyterian church on the hill above town places the photograph between 1863 and 1869, the year the school was built next to the church). Businesses included a meat market, a candy store, several saloons, and a post office. The false fronts of many of the buildings on Main Street are clearly visible.

This view of Black Hawk during the same 1863–1869 period, looking up Gregory Street toward Central City, offers a good view of the buildings on Gregory and the western end of Main Street. Of the buildings seen in this picture, only the church still stands. Portions of Mountain City, which grew up around Gregory Diggings, are visible in the upper left part of the photograph.

This mid-1860s view of Mountain City, the site of John Gregory's diggings, shows how Central City and Black Hawk had grown in a few short years. The wooden buildings on the hill above the Gregory Store are hard rock mines; the towers housed sheave wheels that lowered men and buckets into the mine shafts. The building to the right of the Gregory Store still stands. Once deep rock mining began, Central City and Black Hawk became major destinations for miners from Wales and the Cornwall area of England, who were highly valued for the deep rock mining skills they had developed there. Between 1870 and 1914, more than 5,000 Cornish immigrants arrived in Gilpin County.

These men prepare to go down a mine shaft in an ore bucket in this late 1860s photograph from one of Central City's mines. The cable and chain at the top of the ore bucket went up to the sheave wheel. Larger mining operations used elevators instead of ore buckets. (Courtesy of Denver Public Library Western History Collection, X-11636.)

This model of a typical Gilpin County shaft mine was built in the 1870s, possibly for display at a national exposition. Miners descended vertically to mine levels through the shafts (the large vertical structures on the left and right). The openings going up from a level were called raises, while the openings going down from a level were called winzes. The county also had adit mines, which were entered horizontally.

9301—In the " Bobtail " Mine, Black Hawk Canyon, Col., U. S. A.

Four miners from the Bobtail Mine in Black Hawk, which was located on the Gregory vein, pose for a photographer inside the mine. This was an unusually wide area in the mine tunnel; most areas where the men worked were not nearly as spacious. The horses and donkeys used in the mines rarely saw the light of day during their working lives.

This photograph offers a better idea of the cramped conditions inside mines. The men on either side of the picture holding hammers drill holes for sticks of dynamite. The method they are using is called single jacking because each man hits the drill he is holding with one hammer while also turning the drill between hits. With double jacking, one man hit the drill while another man turned it.

17

This image captures the use of hydraulic equipment in the Chicago Carr Mine. The introduction of the hydraulic drill allowed mines to lay off nearly three-quarters of their hand drillers. The drill used air to clean out the drill holes, forcing miners to breath in silica dust and causing the deadly complaint known as miner's consumption. After 1890, the use of water instead of air alleviated the problem.

RAISE NO. 1. 300T OF 3600T OF 700 FT
LEVEL VEIN OF ORE 5 FEET WIDE

These miners work in a very tight raise of the 700-foot level of the Coeur d'Alene Mine above Central City. The ore bucket that they are filling sits on a set of wheels so that they can roll it back to the shaft in order to be raised to the surface.

The crew poses inside the Coeur d'Alene Shaft House above Central City in this photograph. The hoist that raised and lowered the buckets is visible in the back of the building, on the right. Everything was steam powered, with steam produced by the boilers, which are on the left but not visible behind the men.

Working above the surface was not necessarily any safer than working in a mine. Deadly accidents could happen anywhere. Charles Richards, the mayor of Central City in 1940, died from copper poisoning after the blasting caps he was working on exploded and lodged copper shavings in his body. The work could also be just as dirty, as seen in this image of men shoveling coal.

Many of Gilpin County's mines, such as the Queen of the West Mine in Chase Gulch, west of Black Hawk, were small operations, employing only a handful of miners. The man and woman in this picture may have been the mine's owners or perhaps the superintendent and his wife. The mine above the Queen of the West is unidentified.

Some of Gilpin County's early mining structures were indeed unusual. Although the name and location of this mine are lost to history, its log construction is certainly uncommon. The irregularly shaped log tower in the center most likely housed the sheave wheel over the shaft. Despite the building's unconventional appearance, the crew happily posed for a photographer.

Miners from the Ute Mine pose proudly with the tools of their trade for this photograph outside the mine building. Prior to the introduction of carbide gas lamps in the early 1900s, miners were issued three candles each day. The three candles would burn for 10 hours, the length of their shift. These men earned about $2 a day for their work.

Although placer mining was largely played out within a few years of Gregory's discovery, it did not disappear entirely. These men are placer mining in the Nevada district, just outside of Central City, with a slightly more sophisticated operation than that used by the first miners. In the background, however, is the building of a much larger hard rock mining operation. This photograph was taken in the 1870s or 1880s.

The Gold Coin Mining Company in the Nevada district employed an unusually large number of miners in its operation. As dirty and dangerous as mining could be, the men were still proud of their work and happily pose for this photograph, with some even holding their tools. The photograph also shows that more than a few children worked the mines as well. Many of these men were probably Welsh or Cornish, highly prized for their underground-mining skills. Their love of singing led to the construction of the Central City Opera House. They also built many of the dry-stack rock walls that are still present in Black Hawk and Central City.

In addition to the Cornish, Gilpin County also had a thriving Chinese community, a member of which is seen here. They occupied the areas known as Dostal Alley in Central City and Cottonwood in Black Hawk. Many of them were engaged in the laundry business, but like the majority of other residents, they also mined. The Chinese were known for working claims that other miners considered no longer profitable.

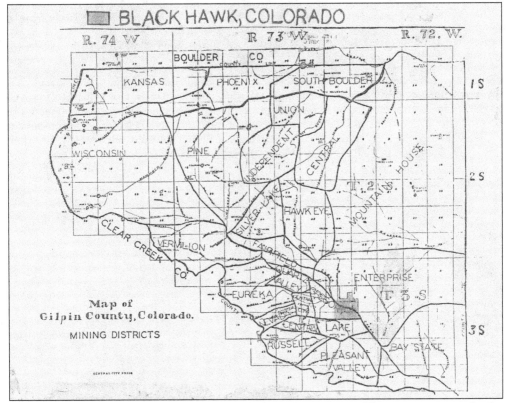

This map shows the mining districts that made up Gilpin County. The gray square marks the location of Black Hawk, and Central City is to the left of it on the map. The Gregory District includes parts of both towns. Detailed claim maps of the districts show that nearly every square inch of ground in the county is part of a mining claim.

Lawyers were especially important in mining towns due to the vast amount of legal issues involved in the finding, owning, and selling of mining claims. Henry Teller (far left) opened his practice in Central City in 1861 and quickly became one of Central City's and Colorado's most prominent citizens. Teller played important roles in politics and the railroad business and served longer than any other Coloradan in the US Senate. His law partner, Chase Withrow, stands in the doorway. Withrow was an important figure in Central City's Masonic Lodge. The law office still stands, but it has been moved three times since Teller first built it.

Law and order was important to Gilpin County's early residents because a stable mining camp helped attract outside investors. Billy Cozens, Central City's second sheriff, built the structure that housed the first county courthouse and the second jail; known as Washington Hall, it still stands on Eureka Street. Prior to building the jail, he was known to sometimes keep prisoners handcuffed to his bed at night.

Washington Hall, built in 1861, is the oldest continually operating government building in Colorado. The first floor held a jail on the left side and the county clerk's office on the right. The second floor was a courtroom that sometimes doubled as a church on Sundays. The bell tower was added in about 1900 when the Central City Fire Department moved into the building. Billy Cozens's house was behind the structure.

Banks were vital in mining towns, where huge amounts of gold regularly changed hands. As the county's banking center, Central City's several establishments included the Mellor Bank and George T. Clark & Company (later First National Bank of Central City). This is the Rocky Mountain National Bank inside the Teller House, pictured in about 1874. The clerks are, from left to right, Thomas Potter, Ed Doris, Richard Brown, and Harry Shuck.

The Rocky Mountain National Bank and the First National Bank of Central City (seen here in its 1874 location on the corner of Main and Eureka Streets) were the longest-lasting and most prominent of Gilpin County's banking houses. The First National Bank building was one of the first reconstructed after the disastrous 1874 fire that destroyed the bank's first home on Main Street.

Harry Lake went to work for the First National Bank of Central City in 1877 as a clerk. He is shown here 50 years later on the day he retired as president in 1927. The door to the bank's vault is visible in the center of the picture. Preservationists moved the base of the teller cage (seen here and in the previous photograph) to the Teller House in the 1930s.

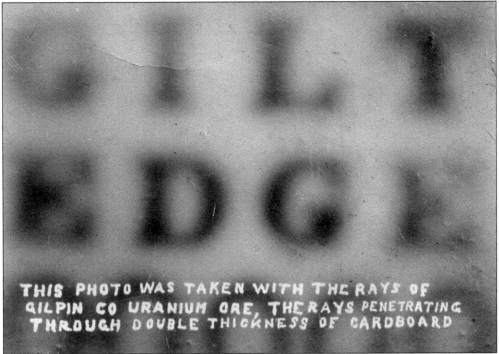

THIS PHOTO WAS TAKEN WITH THE RAYS OF
GILPIN CO URANIUM ORE, THE RAYS PENETRATING
THROUGH DOUBLE THICKNESS OF CARDBOARD

Miners found the first known uranium deposits in the United States at the Wood Mine in Central City in 1871. Over the next 40 years, more than 122,000 tons of pitchblende shipped from the Wood, Calhoun, Kirk, and other area mines, with some of it going to Marie Curie for her experiments. A photographer used uranium to take this picture of a packing crate through two layers of cardboard.

Black Hawk, known as the "City of Mills," was relatively flat compared to Central City, making it ideal land for mills and smelters. Ore wagons or railroad cars would dump ore into the tops of the buildings, where it would go through several stages of processing to recover the gold. Smelters, which used chemicals to process sulfide ores, joined the mills with the 1867 opening of Nathaniel Hill's Boston & Colorado smelter.

Although the name of this Black Hawk mill is unknown, this photograph shows the ore carts dumping the ore inside the top of the building. Once inside, it was crushed and separated, and the gold was extracted. The gold was removed near the bottom, while the waste rock was hauled out of the bottom level and dumped in huge tailings piles, many of which are still visible today.

The mill buildings were essentially giant sheds that housed stamp mills, which crushed ore between opposing sets of hammers, making it easier to extract the gold. California mining man Eben Smith partnered with banker Jerome Chaffee to bring the first stamp mill to Gilpin County in 1860, and their use soon increased dramatically. This photograph shows a pair of five-stamp mills in operation. Some had as many as 80 stamps.

Bela S. Buell's Gregory-Buell mine and mill was one of the largest in Black Hawk and Central City; Buell once delivered 644 ounces of gold to the Rocky Mountain National Bank. The ruins of his stone mill structure (to the right of the wooden building) still stand. The Ontario Mine is at the top of the hill on the right, and below it is the Next President Mine.

The Coeur d'Alene Mine above Central City was unusual for its time. With the exception of dynamite storage, the entire operation—from boilers to machine shop—was under one roof, something many mines tried to avoid so that an explosion or other catastrophe in one area did not destroy everything. The mine was also owned by a woman named Catharine Cameron. The shaft bottomed out at 700 feet.

The Gold Coin Mining Company, located outside of Central City in the Nevada district, was another large mining operation. The large pile to the right of the picture is a tailings pile, made up of waste rock from the mine. These still dot the hills around Black Hawk and Central City today. The mine above the Gold Coin is the California, which, at over 3,000 feet deep, was the deepest in Gilpin County.

The Teller House, opened in 1872, was the first brick hotel in Central City, and it proved to outsiders that the town meant business. It cost nearly $100,000 to build; Henry Teller put up $30,000, securing his name on the building. It cost another $30,000 to furnish. With rooms costing $3 or $4 per night and indoor bathrooms, the hotel was considered the finest in Colorado for many years.

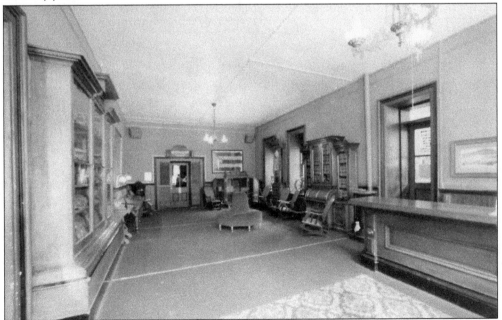

Although this picture of the Teller House's lobby was taken in the 1980s, the interior of the building was remarkably unchanged from the 1870s. Visitors staying at the hotel when it was still in operation in the 1960s even suggested that the beds in the rooms were just uncomfortable enough to have possibly been the originals. Much of the furniture seen in this picture was original to the hotel.

Black Hawk also had a hotel, the Colorado House, owned by miner Patrick Murphy and his wife, Margaret. It was located on Main Street, about where the Gilpin Hotel now stands. Wooden hotels were typical of Gilpin County's early establishments, but they were susceptible to fires and did not suggest permanence, problems that brick hotels such as the Teller House solved.

The owners, staff, and occupants of the Colorado House posed for the camera in the early 1870s. As frequently happened with wooden hotels, the Colorado House was completely destroyed by fire sometime in the 1880s. Unlike Central City, Black Hawk escaped from fires that caused widespread destruction, which gave it an interesting mixture of wood buildings with false fronts sitting next to impressive brick structures.

32

GILPIN HOTEL BLACK HAWK COLO.

Black Hawk never truly adopted one building style in response to disastrous fires the way neighboring Central City did. Owners simply replaced the destroyed building with a new one in the style of their choosing. After the Colorado House burned down, the Gilpin Hotel replaced it as the premier establishment on Black Hawk's Main Street in the late 1800s. Although not as large as the Teller House in Central City, the Gilpin quickly joined it as one of the finest hotels in Colorado. It remained in operation as a hotel and/or bar into the 1980s.

Central City in about 1870 (before the Teller House was built) had grown considerably since the days when it was nothing more than log cabins. This view looks toward the north end of Main Street; the Concert Hall and Billiard Room at the end of the street is next to the Montana Theater. Henry Teller's house is the large white structure at the left side of the picture.

Looking south down Central City's Main Street in about 1873 provided further proof of the town's growth. Central City boasted two bookstores, a drugstore, several dry-goods stores, at least two banks, several churches, two theaters, and an integrated public school. Nearly every Main Street building in this picture would be destroyed in the 1874 fire.

Two

FROM MINING CAMP
TO HOME
1874–1900

Black Hawk and Central City remained economically and politically powerful as they continued to grow in the 1870s. When Colorado became a state in 1876, its first two US senators, Henry Teller and Jerome Chaffee, and its first US representative, James Belford, were either residents of Central City or had strong business ties to the community. The towns could claim to have two of the earliest public schools in the state. The schools were also among the earliest integrated in the state after Henry Teller threatened to sue Central City when it closed its school for black children and refused to provide an alternative. The Catholics operated a private school as well, St. Aloysius Academy, where no student was turned away because a family could not afford tuition. When the train arrived in Black Hawk in 1872, it quickly replaced the wagon roads of the 1860s as the preferred method of transportation between the two towns and Golden and Denver. Baseball and theater were popular recreational activities; Central City's Stars baseball team even won the territorial championship in 1869 and 1870. The Central City Opera House opened in 1878 and attracted theatergoers from around Colorado. Several newspapers called the county home, including the *Tri-Weekly Miner's Register*, the *Gilpin Observer*, and the *Weekly Register-Call* (the oldest newspaper in the state after the demise of the *Rocky Mountain News* in 2009). Residents had a wide array of clothing, grocery, jewelry, and hardware stores in which to shop. Churches were an integral part of the communities, and between Black Hawk and Central City, the Catholic, Presbyterian, Methodist, Episcopal, Congregational, and Baptist denominations were represented. Saloons and billiard halls were extremely popular in both towns (each could, at times, claim more than a dozen), and many doubled as early churches and schools. The two communities also enjoyed well-regulated red-light districts; Black Hawk's was based at the Toll Gate Saloon, and Central City's was found at two houses on Pine Street. By the 1890s, Black Hawk and Central City had most assuredly become home for the people who lived there.

This stereoview card shows the Forks on Clear Creek, situated near the present-day intersection of Highways 6 and 119. This was one of several stopping points on the journey between Golden and Black Hawk once the narrow- (three-foot) gauge Colorado Central (later the Colorado & Southern) train route went into operation in December 1872. The train reduced a journey that had once taken several days to just four hours.

This photograph from the 1880s shows that Black Hawk's Main Street had changed quite a bit since 1859. The Black Hawk School, built between 1869 and 1870, sits on the hill next to the Presbyterian church. To the right of the photograph is the train yard for the Colorado & Southern/Colorado Central Railroad and the Gilpin Tram.

Looking up Gregory Street toward Central City provides further evidence of the changes that Black Hawk had undergone. Here, a train crosses the 1873-built trestle over Gregory Street. The trestle became a Black Hawk landmark and was a popular place for people to take photographs. The school and church are in the upper right of the photograph.

Five women pose for a photographer on the Gregory Street trestle in about 1915. The Black Hawk School and Presbyterian church are visible in the background. Views of the trestle were a favorite shot for photographers for as long as the structure stood, especially if they could catch a train crossing it.

Prior to the construction of the first railroad, horses and wagons were the only method of transportation in Black Hawk and Central City. Consequently, livery stables were very important businesses. Even after the arrival of the train in 1870s, the stables retained their value, as it was often faster to ride a horse between the two towns than take the train. Williams Stables (above), shown here in the 1920s, still stands in Central City. Oscar Williams, the second generation of the Williams family to own it, stands to the right of the Dalmatian. Black Hawk's Livery Stables (below) was owned by the very prominent Blake family, members of which are seen posing in front of it.

The teachers and students of the Black Hawk School pose outside of the building for a photographer in about 1900. The two mine buildings in the background were reminders of the dominance of the mining business in Black Hawk and Central City. The steeple on the church had already been removed by the time this picture was taken and would not be restored until the 1990s.

Central City had two public schools—the stone school (with the bell tower) was built in 1870 and became the high school in 1900, and the brick Clark School in front of it, built in 1900, served as the elementary school. As the population in Central City and Black Hawk dropped, all students went to the high school in Central City. The schools remained in use until the mid-1960s.

The students of Central City's stone school, including three black children, posed for this photograph in 1871. Prior to the stone school's opening, the city had closed a separate school for black children, located on Eureka Street, because so few children attended it. When the city refused to provide another such school, Henry Teller threatened to file a lawsuit, which resulted in the stone school being integrated from the day it opened. The man standing to the left side of the photograph is Horace Hale, the first principal of the Central City School. He went on to become president of the University of Colorado from 1887 to 1892. Hale is considered the father of Colorado's system of education because of his hard work in establishing it.

The teachers from Central City's stone school pose outside of the front doors of the building, and although no date is given, this image was probably captured in the late 1870s or early 1880s. Pictured from left to right are "James A. Smith, Miss Glew, Miss Stevens, Miss Strain, Miss Robinson," and "Miss Brooks." The teachers were paid between $50 and $80 a month, while the principal was paid $150.

Students pose outside of the stone school in Central City with their teacher in 1888. The door on the left side of the picture was sealed up when an expansion was added onto the rear building in the mid-1890s to create two more rooms. The building still stands and has been home to the Gilpin History Museum since 1970.

In addition to public schools, Central City had several private schools as well. The Sisters of Charity opened St. Aloysius Academy in 1875 for both day and boarding students. The school was not financially successfully, and in 1877, the Sisters of Charity turned over its operation to the Sisters of St. Joseph, who changed its name to St. Patrick's Academy. To reach the school, a person had to climb a 240-foot-long flight of stairs from Pine Street below. The school remained in operation under the Sisters of St. Joseph until 1917. After being severely damaged in a fire set by vandals in 1936, it was torn down.

St. James Methodist Church on Eureka Street in Central City is the oldest Protestant congregation in Colorado. Construction of the building began in 1863 and moved slowly; by November 1868, the congregation was meeting in the finished basement. The stained-glass windows were installed in 1871, and the building was completed in 1872 at a cost of $42,000.

The children of St. James pose inside the church sometime in 1899. In May of that year, a special pipe organ would be installed in the area where the children are standing. The organ could be powered by water or electricity, or it could be hand pumped. Both the organ and the church remain in use today.

Fr. J.P. Machbeuf performed the first Catholic Mass in Central City in November 1860; six years later, construction began on a brick church, but money ran out with only the basement walls finished. Parishioners put a roof over the basement in 1874 and called it St. Patrick's. In 1892, the basement was torn down, and St. Mary's of the Assumption (pictured) was built in its place.

The priests and altar boys of St. Mary's pose inside the church in the late 1890s or early 1900s. Much of the altar area still looks the same today, but many of the stained-glass windows have been replaced with windows donated by members of the congregation to honor their relatives.

St. Paul's Episcopal Church was organized in 1860 and originally occupied a wooden building on Lawrence Street that was destroyed in the fire of 1873. The granite building on First High Street next to the stone school was finished in December 1873 at a cost of $12,000. Until the church got the bell from Christ Church in Nevadaville in 1926, the school bell was used to call people to services.

The fire of 1873 destroyed many other buildings on Lawrence Street in addition to the first St. Paul's. Raynold's Court, the brick structure below and to the left of the school, was erected in 1863 and is one of the oldest commercial buildings in Colorado. The large two-story building below and to the right of the school was the Congregational church. (Courtesy of History Colorado, F-6729.)

This Presbyterian church was built in 1872 on a lot between the Teller House and what would be the Central City Opera House on Eureka Street. In 1922, the portion of the flume running between Academy Hill and the Teller House that was under the church caved in, and after Central City deemed the building unsafe, it was torn down.

In addition to the Presbyterian church on the hill above town, Black Hawk also had its own Methodist church. The original building was on Swede Hill, but it was destroyed by a flood in 1890. The congregation rebuilt the church on Gregory Street. It currently houses an Evangelical Free Church congregation.

By the mid-1870s, Black Hawk and Central City had firmly established themselves as permanent, law-abiding towns through their mining activities, banks, newspapers, schools, churches, and theaters. The towns could also claim the services of two highly trained doctors, brothers Abraham "Guy" and Theophilus L. Ashbaugh (pictured), who arrived in 1879. Between the two of them, the brothers served as county coroner for more than 30 years.

Fire devastated Central City on May 21, 1874. In three hours, it destroyed most of Main Street between Spring and High Streets; the brick Teller House and Masonic Block stopped it from spreading west, while the Raynold's Block prevented it from going east. Residents first blamed the fire, which started in the Chinese section of Dostal Alley, on a religious ceremony. However, the likely cause was a chimney fire.

Fire insurance policies paid $114,533 toward the loss—estimated at between $500,000 and $750,000—caused by the 1874 fire. Central City ordered that all new construction in town use brick to lessen the damage from any future fires. By the time this photograph was taken in early 1875, Main Street had been rebuilt by its unfazed residents.

This is another view of Central City's rebuilt Main Street, taken in about 1875. The Teller House and Masonic Block (located across Eureka Street from the hotel) are in the center of the picture. The small stone building above the Westman & Newell store on the left side of the picture is St. Patrick's Catholic Church.

The miners who were Gilpin County's first residents were satisfied by the goods available from the mining supply stores that existed to serve them, but a larger population required more than these simple shops. By the mid-1870s, Central City and Black Hawk residents had their choice of dozens of stores in which to shop. Central City's Temple of Fashion was the preeminent clothing store, but there were also several jewelry stores, the Quiller & Gabardi Dry Goods Store, Jenkins-McKay Hardware in Central City, Clark Hardware in Black Hawk, and many others. Aime Rapin opened his jewelry store in Central City (above) in about 1896 and soon had stores all over the state. The Brzago Store (below) was a dry-goods store in Black Hawk.

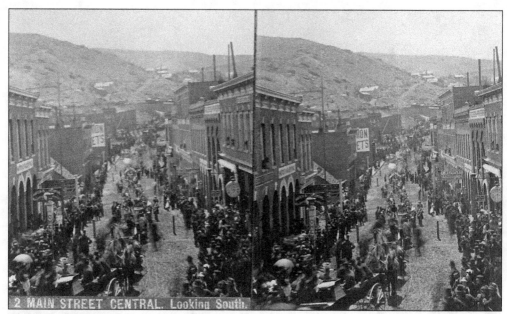

This view looking south on Central City's rebuilt Main Street was captured by photographer Charles Weitfle in the late 1870s. The "C. Weitfle" sign on the right side of the street marks his studio; he was famous for making these stereoview cards. The first sign sticking out on the left is for the Hatch & Valentine Jewelry Store.

Armory Hall, located at the intersection of Main and Nevada Streets in Central City, was among the first buildings constructed after the 1874 fire. It housed the 475-seat Belvidere Theater, which was supposed to be the finest theater in Central City. A standing-room-only crowd on opening night, however, convinced residents that they needed a bigger theater and led to plans for the Central City Opera House.

Built in 1877 at a cost of
$20,000, all of which was
donated by the people of
Central City, the Central City
Opera House was designed by
Robert Roeschlaub, Colorado's
first licensed architect. After
it opened in 1878, the opera
house was home to plays,
operas, boxing matches,
political rallies, and high school
graduations. Its theatrical
productions made Central City
a cultural center in Colorado.

When it first opened, the Central City Opera House could seat about 750 people between the main floor and balcony. The building boasted perfect acoustics, and even today, performers use no sound equipment inside it. The orchestra pit was fairly unusual in that most of it was underneath the stage rather than in front of it; the pit could hold up to 50 musicians.

Central City resident Henry Teller was president of the Colorado Central Railroad when it completed the line to Black Hawk in 1872. He insisted that the train also had to go to Central City, but it was no easy task and took six years to become a reality. In 1878, the same year the opera house opened, a photographer captured this picture of the first train to reach Central City. Builders had to put in so many switchbacks to get up the extra 500 feet in elevation from Black Hawk that, for many years, it was still faster to take a horse or stagecoach between the two towns than it was to ride the train.

Looking south down Main Street in Central City past the California Fruit Store, a train can be seen leaving Central City. The Central City Train Depot was located on Spring Street and was, in reality, quite small when compared to other train stations of the time. The mine on the hill above the train is unidentified.

The engineer stopped the train somewhere on its journey between Black Hawk and Central City so that the photographer could take this picture of it. The group of men standing outside the train is likely the crew. The passengers have gathered at the windows of the cars, not wanting to miss their chance to be photographed.

In 1886, businessmen incorporated the Gilpin Tramway Company to operate a two-foot-gauge tram to haul ore from Central City's mines to Black Hawk's mills. The unusual two-foot gauge was chosen because of its low construction costs, cheaper equipment costs, and ability to navigate tight curves. At its peak, it covered 26.46 miles. The tram is shown here at its engine house outside of Black Hawk in about 1905.

A Gilpin Tram shay engine and cars are seen going past a mine building in Black Hawk in this photograph from the late 1890s. The larger Colorado & Southern car sitting on the tracks in front of the mine building offers an idea of how much bigger the regular railroad cars were and why the tram was useful for transporting ore.

While Central City dealt with fires, Black Hawk had to deal with frequent flooding. Water from rainstorms or snowmelt would rush down the hills from Central City and hit the relatively flatland of Black Hawk, causing major damage. There were occasions when people deliberately tried to start fires in Black Hawk, but the floods were far more damaging. This is Gregory Street, probably after the 1894 flood.

Residents gather outside of the grocery store on Gregory Street in Black Hawk after the 1913 flood to survey the damage. The Colorado & Southern trestle, crossing above Gregory Street, is visible at the top of the picture. One of Gilpin County's famous dry-stack rock walls, built by the Cornish miners who lived in Black Hawk and Central City, is visible below the trestle.

Gilpin County residents could always count on their neighbors in a disaster. Residents turned out to repair flood damage along Black Hawk's Main Street when this picture was taken in 1910. The Colorado & Southern laid temporary tracks up Main Street so that train cars could haul away the debris. The Gilpin Hotel is the brick building on the right.

Although Black Hawk sustained the majority of flood damage in Gilpin County, Central City did see its share, as evidenced in this picture of the 1914 flood. The floodwaters even managed to toss about heavy mining equipment, which the team of horses in the upper right corner of the picture is probably waiting to move. This view looks down Gregory Gulch toward Black Hawk.

Flooding also caused the worst mining disaster in Gilpin County history. On August 29, 1895, water from the lower levels of the Fiske Mine in Black Hawk broke through to the neighboring Americus and Sleepy Hollow Mines, drowning 14 men. It took until October to recover all of the bodies. This photograph shows a funeral for one of the victims at St. Mary's.

In this photograph looking across Black Hawk (the church and school are in the lower left), from left to right, the Fisk, Americus, and Sleepy Hollow Mines are the three mines that run diagonally uphill across the center of the picture. The eastern end of Central City (formerly Mountain City) is visible in the center of the photograph on the right.

With fires and other disasters so prevalent, both Black Hawk and Central City had very active fire departments. Here, the Black Hawk Fire Department's running team poses in front of the building that served as city hall and the fire station in 1903. In addition to its importance during fires, running teams also competed in annual competitions to see which department's team could run fastest.

Central City's fire department poses in front of its station at Armory Hall on Nevada Street in this photograph by A.M. Thomas. The fire department occupied this space until 1900, when they moved into the former jail space in Washington Hall. It moved a third time, to a building on Lawrence Street, in the 1970s.

Despite a sometimes hard life, Gilpin County's residents found plenty of time for pleasure. This photograph shows a game in progress at Central City's baseball field, located at the intersection of Main, Nevada, and Spring Streets. The field also served as a city park, rodeo grounds, and ice-skating rink. The Coeur d'Alene Mine and St. Aloysius Academy are visible on the hill above it.

Baseball was an enormously popular sport in Gilpin County, and most of the towns had their own teams, though some were better at the game than others. Central City's most famous team was the two-time territorial-championship-winning Stars, while Black Hawk's team was the Lilies. The Stars usually beat the Lilies, winning one game 62-24. This photograph shows Central City's team in 1900.

By the 1910s, Gilpin County had just one baseball team, the Gilpin County Mines. The Mines team played all over the state, but they never quite gained the fame that the Central City Stars had once enjoyed. They did, however, have a women's team in addition to the men's team.

One of the Gilpin County Mines women players poses with fans. Among the most notable baseball fans in Central City was Lou Bunch, one of the town's madams. Fans at Sunday games always noticed Bunch's carriage parked at the baseball field and the madam and her girls sitting in the stands, cheering for the home team. It was a rare venture outside of the red-light district for them.

After being scattered in various buildings for years, Central City's red-light district was moved to the end of Pine Street in the 1880s. Residents tolerated the women provided that they stayed in their part of town. They were based in the two houses in the upper left corner of this photograph, and their location, a block away from St. Mary's Church, led to numerous jokes and unverifiable stories.

Central City's last (and most famous) madam was Lou Bunch. She started her career as one of Madam Mattie Silks's girls in Denver in the 1870s before becoming a madam herself. Bunch operated her house in Central City, with between two and four girls, from 1899 to 1915, when approaching statewide Prohibition put most brothels out of business. (Courtesy of History Colorado, Mazzula Collection, FF1273.)

This panoramic view of Central City in about 1900 shows how the town had grown from its earliest days. The train depot is in the lower left, and to its right is the baseball field. Above the baseball field, in the center of the picture, are the town's two brothels, and above them is the Coeur d'Alene. To the right of the Coeur d'Alene is St. Aloysius Academy, and below it to

the right is St. Mary's. Main Street is in the lower right corner, and the Teller House is visible just above the end of Main Street. Above it are St. James and the new courthouse. With a few exceptions, Central City still looks very much like this photograph today.

GILPIN COUNTY COURT HOUSE — CENTRAL CITY, COLO.

As Gilpin County grew, government officials decided that they needed a bigger courthouse than the aging Washington Hall. They first attempted to buy the financially struggling Central City Opera House for use as a courthouse in 1882, but angry residents forced them to give up that plan. It took another 17 years, but the residents of Gilpin County finally built a new courthouse on Eureka Street in Central City. Construction began in 1899, and the building opened in 1900. It cost $30,000 to build and another $2,000 to furnish. The courthouse included a new jail in the basement, with separate cell areas for men and women.

This photograph looks at Marchant Street in Black Hawk in about 1900. Central City and Black Hawk began electrifying their towns in about 1880 and were almost fully electrified by 1900. The service was not always reliable at first, however, many buildings chose to use combination gas-and-electric lights; one example of which can still be seen in the Teller House today. The Gilpin County Light, Heating & Power Company's building is visible in the lower right corner. One structure from the old power company remains in Central City, now serving as the elevator shaft for the parking garage at the Reserve Casino.

This panoramic photograph shows Black Hawk's Main Street, as well as the northern end of the town, in about 1900. The third house from the left is the famous Lace House, which would become a popular tourist attraction in the 1970s because of its distinctive gingerbread trim. The Toll Gate Saloon, home to Black Hawk's red-light district, is on the left side of the picture, to the

right of the bend in Clear Creek between the two light-colored buildings. As was the case with
Central City, Black Hawk's red-light district was kept segregated from the decent part of town.
The long building in the foreground is the state-owned ore-sampling works. The train tracks to
Central City are on Bobtail Hill behind the houses.

For more than 40 years, mining had made Black Hawk and Central City household names throughout Colorado and even the United States. Ulysses S. Grant had visited the communities three times, including twice as president. Residents hoping to impress Grant had even placed $20,000 worth of silver bars on the front steps of the Teller House for him to walk on; they chose silver because gold was just too common a sight in Central City. But, as the 19th century came to a close, the glory days for crews like the one seen here, posing outside of the Ironact Mine in Russell Gulch, were quickly coming to a close.

Three

FROM HOME TO ALMOST GHOST TOWN
1901–1931

By the beginning of the 20th century, Black Hawk and Central City were no longer the economic and political powerhouses they had once been. The mining boom had long since moved on to other places in Colorado—Boulder in the early 1870s, Leadville and Aspen in the later 1870s and 1880s, and Cripple Creek in the 1890s—and people who depended on mining for their survival left Gilpin County for the new hot spots. In some cases, they even took their houses with them. With the hillsides in and around Black Hawk and Central City stripped bare of trees for the mines, people had to have lumber for their homes shipped in at great cost when building in the 1860s; when they left town, they simply disassembled the houses and took them along. Mining in Gilpin County was by no means dead, but it was nowhere near as active or profitable as it had been in the 1860s and 1870s. When the United States entered World War I in 1917, mining ground to a halt, and large numbers of people abandoned Black Hawk and Central City for Denver, Golden, Idaho Springs, and other bigger cities. The two towns seemed to be caught in a vicious cycle; as businesses closed, more people left, and then as more people left, more businesses closed. Statewide Prohibition in 1916 even forced the closure of Central City's one remaining brothel. With the start of National Prohibition in 1919, Gilpin County's abandoned mine buildings became havens for bootleggers until the county sheriff started ordering such buildings burned down in order to prevent the problem. The county's mine shafts also became convenient dumping grounds for some victims of Denver's occasionally messy gang wars. By the 1920s, the once-grand Central City Opera House operated as a barely profitable movie theater, while the once-glamorous Teller House was essentially a boardinghouse whose residents used the atrium as their trash dump. But, for those who remained, Black Hawk and Central City were home, and they went on with life as best they could.

By the early 1900s, though Gilpin County's brightest mining days were in the past and its power was fading, it still occupied a strong place in the memories of many. When Denver hosted the 1908 Democratic National Convention in July, planners went all out entertaining delegates, with events including snowball fights with trucked-in snow, a visit to the new Lakeside Amusement Park in Denver, and Indian dances and other performances. The festivities also included a visit to Gilpin County, where delegates toured mining sites and rode on the Gilpin Tram. The delegates also had lunch at the Central City Opera House, where they posed for this photograph.

Tourism briefly became a minor business in Central City in the 1910s, and the Gilpin Tram temporarily saw more service as a passenger train than as an ore-hauling train during that time. This group of tourists is on the tram in about 1917, shortly before the tram's tracks were torn up and all of the equipment was sold for scrap.

Black Hawk and Central City also became popular movie locations. Tom Mix, seen here in front of Williams Stables on Eureka Street in Central City, filmed three movies (including *Why the Sheriff Is a Bachelor* and *Western Hearts*) in and around the towns in 1910 and 1911 for the Selig-Polyscope Picture Company. He was almost killed when he fell down a mountain doing a stunt for one of them.

Mix also starred in a Labor Day 1911 rodeo at the baseball field in Central City. He is the man on horseback wearing a dark hat and white shirt with no vest. Mix's appearance in Central City began a century of movie and television productions using Black Hawk and Central City as filming locations.

Three women pose on a Colorado & Southern train car in this photograph from 1926. Behind them on the left is the Iron City Mill, which was just below Black Hawk near Silver Creek Gulch. The very impressive mill was demolished in the 1930s. After service steadily decreased through the 1920s and 1930s, the last train to Black Hawk ran in 1941.

As this image shows, Black Hawk's buildings were beginning to show their age by the 1920s. The Gilpin Hotel is in the center of the picture, and the train station is on the right. The train tracks are in less than ideal condition in this photograph as well. The absence of the Gilpin Tram's third rail on the tracks dates this view to sometime after 1917.

This view of Gregory Street in Black Hawk in about 1926 also shows the aging appearance of the town. The school on the hill was still in business, but only as an elementary school. High school–aged students went to the stone school in Central City, which, with voter approval, became the Gilpin County Combined High School in 1921.

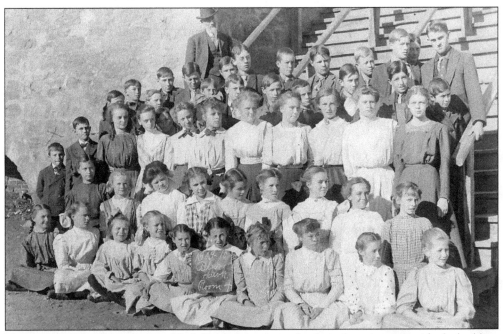

The students from Room 4 of the Black Hawk School pose for their class picture outside the building during the 1909–1910 academic year. The number of students in the school was decreasing as both Black Hawk and Central City continued their downward slide. Before too long, a photograph of every student in the school would show a smaller group than the one grade seen here.

Conditions in Central City were not much better in the 1920s. The iron fire shutters on the exterior of the Teller House had been a sign of the building's virtually fireproof status. By the time this picture was taken in the mid-1920s, only a few shutters on the west side of the structure remained. By the outbreak of World War II, even these would be gone.

Once a rooming house for miners, by the 1920s, the Granite Block on Eureka Street in Central City was a service station, complete with a gas pump in front. Cars were enormously popular among Black Hawk and Central City residents, but not until the 1950s would Highways 6 and 119, along the old train route through Clear Creek Canyon, connect the towns to Golden and Denver.

Residents continued to enjoy many of their traditional amusements despite the tough economic times in the 1910s and 1920s. The hose-cart races on Central City's Main Street remained a popular pastime. This photograph shows Central City's 1924 hose team on Main Street; the team came in second and won $25. Main Street still looked much as it had since being rebuilt in 1874.

Students at Central City's schools continued with their normal course work as well. In this photograph from the late 1930s or early 1940s, students at the Gilpin County Combined High School are checking scientific instruments (possibly weather related) in the front yard of the school. The Clark School, the city's elementary school, is visible in front of them.

Residents began to embrace their history in the 1920s and 1930s. Central City had been home to Colorado's first Masonic Lodge, built in 1859 near where the Buell Mill stood. In 1933, the Masons unveiled a monument marking the lodge's original location. In 2011, they dedicated another monument on the site in honor of the 150th anniversary of the lodge. Central City's and Nevadaville's lodges remain active today.

The monument to John Gregory's 1859 discovery, erected by the State Historical Society of Colorado, was slightly less grand. In this photograph, probably from the 1920s, a group of men pose around the simple wooden sign. As the marker notes, more than $20 million worth of gold had been mined from the Gregory lode by then. Ruins marked the area that had once been crammed with mine buildings and stores.

Four

RISING FROM THE ASHES
1932–1990

As mining continued its decline in the late 1920s and early 1930s, many in Central City and Black Hawk sought ways to revive their dying communities. Tourism seemed to be the answer, but it was hard to draw people to the mountain towns. Dr. William Muchow, a Chicago dentist, sparked a small revival in mining and interest in Central City when he opened the Glory Hole Mine to, in part, supply gold for his dental practice. But mining alone was not enough to draw crowds. In late 1931, a group of women, including Anne Evans, University of Denver English professor Ida Kruse McFarlane, and socialite Minnie Crook, decided to reopen the Central City Opera House as a theater. They restored the long-closed building and, on July 16, 1932, staged a production of *Camille* starring silent-movie actress Lillian Gish. With the opera house's success, those who had wanted to revive Central City had a hook to get people into town, and other tourism-based businesses quickly followed. Bars proliferated, and the Toll Gate, the Gold Nugget, the Glory Hole Tavern, and the Teller House's Face Bar (home of the infamous painting *The Face on the Barroom Floor*), were packed with tourists during summers. Rock shops, antique shops, candy stores, and restaurants like the Gilded Garter were also filled with visitors. And, of course, gambling became a big draw. Nearly every bar in town had at least a few slot machines, while some bigger operations, such as the Monte Carlo and the Reno Club, offered more gambling options. The Monte Carlo was operated by the Denver mob family the Smaldones, who gained respect and convinced city officials to turn a blind eye to their activities by investing in infrastructure upgrades and funding a hot-lunch program for the schools. The police frequently conducted raids, but lookouts posted along the route and clever tricks on the part of casino operators and their employees kept the operation safe. While Black Hawk entered into a steep decline during this period, Central City had been reborn as a major tourist destination.

Inscription

To

Dr. WM. MARK MUCHOW

July 20. 1929

Chain O'Mines

Whose Faith,

Vision and

Courage brought

back a dead town

and united

the Patch.

The Little Kingdom
of golden
Gilpin County, Colo.
also known among
mining men as the
"Richest Square Mile
on Earth", was

Discovered by
John H. Gregory
May 6th, 1859.

Over 1000 Mines
in this famous
district are now
united under the
CHAIN O'MINES
Inc.
Chicago

Dr. William Muchow, a Chicago dentist who some claim invented dental floss, began purchasing mines in Gilpin County in 1929. Although the number of mines he owned was far less than the 1,000 claimed in this self-promotional postcard, he did employ hundreds of miners, convincing people to once again pay attention to the towns of Black Hawk and Central City.

Some said that miners pulled over $200 million in gold from the Glory Hole before it closed in 1959; others argued that Muchow made most of that money from investors. Beyond dispute was the drawing power of the Glory Hole, which became a major tourist attraction and was visited by thousands. A glory hole mine was created by caving in the roof of a mine tunnel while also digging down from above.

One unfortunate side effect of the Glory Hole was the tailings piles it created, burying Central City's Mission-style train depot. In this picture from about 1932, the tailings from the mine are just beginning to creep up the sides of the building (in the lower right corner). One legend says Muchow put the contents of the depot in boxes in case someone wanted to dig it up one day.

Muchow's Glory Hole revived interest in Central City, but it took restoring the opera house to truly revitalize the town. A group of women under the leadership of Anne Evans and Ida Kruse McFarlane formed the Central City Opera House Association in 1931 and set out to restore and reopen the building, seen here in the 1920s. The Teller House is just beyond it.

Anne Evans, daughter of John Evans (Colorado's second territorial governor and cofounder of the University of Denver), was instrumental in reopening the opera house. Her reputation as a persistent fundraiser led many friends to quickly write a check whenever they saw her approaching them on the street. She is seen here in 1938 with Robert Edmond Jones, artistic director of the opera. (Courtesy of David Forsyth.)

Ida Kruse McFarlane, who taught English at the University of Denver, was also the daughter-in-law of opera house owner Peter McFarlane. She helped convince the McFarlane family to donate the opera house to the university after Peter's death. The remnants of St. Aloysius Academy became a memorial to her after her death in 1940.

The Central City Opera House Association paid for the building's restoration by selling naming rights to the chairs inside. For $100, people could have the name of a Colorado pioneer engraved on one of the seat backs. Numerous people took advantage of the opportunity, and many of the names on the chairs are those of once prominent Gilpin County residents. The sales raised over $15,000 to fund repairs, which included a new roof and restoration of the original plaster ceiling. Although Colorado Springs artist Allen True gets credit for restoring the ceiling, Central City artist Paschal Quackenbush did most of the work. He also restored the ceiling and the muse murals inside the Teller House bar.

On July 16, 1932, the Central City Opera House reopened for the first time since January 1, 1927, with the play *Camille*, starring silent-movie actress Lillian Gish. The reopening drew hundreds of people from the surrounding communities, including Denver, and attracted nationwide attention with live radio broadcasts on opening night. (Courtesy of David Forsyth.)

Lillian Gish, on stage in the opera house as Camille in this photograph, delighted audiences. Critics, however, blasted the play, arguing that Gish's sweet and innocent public image from her movie career disqualified her for such a racy role. To prove its success, the director took the show from Central City to Broadway, where audiences were not nearly as kind, and it ultimately failed.

With the opera house reopened, the Central City Opera House Association became interested in restoring other buildings, including the Teller House. The Teller House became home to one of the town's most famous landmarks, *The Face on the Barroom Floor*, painted by Denver artist Herndon Davis in 1936. The face is his wife, Juanita, but whether he painted it as a joke or a serious work remains hotly debated. (Courtesy of David Forsyth.)

The Face became so famous that annual recitals of Antoine d'Arcy's 1887 poem "The Face on the Barroom Floor" by actor Charles Young took place on Main Street as an expected part of opening-day festivities each summer. *The Face on the Barroom Floor* painting became so well known that the Central City Opera even commissioned composer Henry Mollicone to write a one-act opera about it in 1978.

Before the construction of Highways 6 and 119 in the 1940s and 1950s, tourists reached Central City by taking the Virginia Canyon Road from Idaho Springs. The road was eventually nicknamed the "Oh My God Road" because of its steep drops and breathtaking scenery. One story credits a friend of Central City bartender and opera house performer Bill Axton with giving the road its name because of the exclamation he let out when he was informed that what he thought were nice bushes along the side of the road were actually the tops of trees from below. Axton's friend was not alone in uttering those words while traveling the road. This busload of tourists is from the late 1920s or early 1930s.

In revived Central City, bars, antique shops, museums, and candy stores flourished. One of the most popular bars was the Glory Hole, which, to Muchow's displeasure, was named after the mine. In this image, singer Mattie Mosch (in white shirt and vest) and owner Emmy Wilson (in hat), granddaughter of Central City pioneer Eben Smith, are in the center of the crowd at the Glory Hole. A portrait of Smith is on the wall. (Courtesy of David Forsyth.)

A small uranium boom in the late 1940s and early 1950s also helped along Central City's revival. Although the second attempt at uranium mining in Gilpin County did not amount to much in the end, many people tried it. A *Denver Post* photographer took this picture of supposedly secret uranium mining activity at the Wood and Calhoun Mines near Central City in April 1953. (Courtesy of David Forsyth.)

Tyler Hall's photograph of the Toll Gate Saloon on Main Street perfectly captures the feel of Central City during the height of its tourist days. The Toll Gate was known for, among other things, the quality of its live music, and several of its best performers released record albums that identified them as being acts seen at the Toll Gate. (Courtesy of Viola Hall Steckel.)

The Gold Coin Saloon, also on Main Street in Central City, was one of the oldest continuously operating bars in Colorado, and its appearance remained virtually unchanged from the day it opened in 1894. Like other such establishments in Central City, its popularity boomed during the height of the tourist revival. Photographer Tyler Hall captured this image during one of its quieter moments. (Courtesy of Viola Hall Steckel.)

With renewed interest in the arts in Central City, the Gilpin County Arts Association opened a gallery on the second floor of Washington Hall on Eureka Street in 1946. Every summer since then, the gallery has exhibited and sold work by local artists, and it remains a popular gathering place for opera patrons before performances. The building is seen here during one of the opera's opening-day parades.

Central City's Main Street in the late 1940s was packed with tourists visiting the town's popular bars and illegal casinos. The Monte Carlo, operated by Denver's infamous crime family the Smaldones is on the right. The Reno Club, visible just beyond it, was another illegal casino. City residents admired the Smaldones for their charitable contributions to the town, but increased police pressure forced them out in the early 1950s.

No visit to Central City was complete without a stop at an antique shop or Springer's Pharmacy, the oldest pharmacy in Colorado by the time this picture was taken in the 1950s. The Mines Hotel, situated at the intersection of Main and Lawrence Streets (seen here in the lower right corner), was owned by the Chain O'Mines Company, which operated the Glory Hole Mine.

Tourists could also see a submarine built in 1898 by Central City engineer Rufus T. Owen. The vessel sank in Missouri Lake (outside of Black Hawk) on its maiden voyage and was pulled from its watery grave in 1944. Housed in a museum on Main Street until 1970, the submarine then spent 40 years in a private collection before going on display again at the Gilpin History Museum in 2011.

Opera boosters made many efforts to recreate the feeling of bygone days, including letting tourists ride a donkey through town during opening-day parades. The parades were meant to signify the opening of opera season, but they drew more than just opera fans. On a typical summer day, people had trouble finding a place to park because Central City was so packed with tourists.

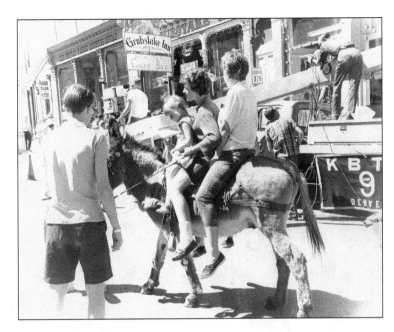

During the parades, another nod to Central City's mining past came in the form of drilling competitions on Main Street. Demonstrating the amazing skill that miners needed in order to hand drill in the days before steam-powered drills, the competitions judged who could drill a hole the fastest, which was somewhat easier on Main Street than inside a cramped and dark mine.

Many famous stars, including Shirley Booth, Beverly Sills, and Christopher Reeve, performed at the Central City Opera House in the summers as New York theater productions traveled the country to escape their non–air-conditioned theaters. Among the most popular, however, was Mae West, starring in *Diamond Lil* in 1949. She had two white limousines at her disposal at all times during her short stay in Central City. (Courtesy of the Axton family.)

A few famous people even took up residence in Central City, including Ozie Waters. Already a radio, movie, and recording star by the time he arrived in the area, Waters also served as a police deputy from 1964 to 1965. He is seen here walking down Main Street in his uniform.

As tourism expanded, Dr. J.M. Newman and his son Ward partnered with Waters to build this recreation of Fort Cody in the old mining town of Gilpin in the late 1950s. The area included a stage for performances, a fire pit, food and concession stands, a fishing pond, and an Indian village. Numerous problems plagued the venture, however, and it lasted only one year. The remains of the fort were bulldozed in 1965.

Fort Cody's builders moved members of a tribe from Idaho to be the residents of the Indian village at the fort. One of the many reasons that Fort Cody failed involved the expense of housing the residents of the Indian village, which turned out to be far more costly than the backers had anticipated.

By the late 1960s, the parades that marked the opening of the summer opera season had become major events, filling Main Street with tourists who saw marching bands, antique cars, hose-cart races, and clowns. The parades were also broadcast on television, drawing even more tourists. The popular Grubstake Inn can be seen here in the upper left, while the Chain O'Mines Hotel is on the right.

Despite the appeal of seeing the "World's Largest Steer," Black Hawk's Main Street in 1957 failed to attract anywhere near the number of visitors that descended on uphill neighbor Central City during the same period. Despite Black Hawk's decline, the Gilpin Hotel, on the right side of the picture, was promoted as one of the oldest hotels in the state and was still open for business.

Looking west up Main Street in Black Hawk provides further evidence of the town's desolation when compared to neighboring Central City. The Gilpin Hotel is on the left; the large building at the end of the row on the right once housed the Stroehle Iron and Boiler Works. The antique shop just past the "This Is It" sign even advertised that it sold junk.

This long view of Black Hawk's Main Street looking toward the elementary school and Presbyterian church shows that, like neighboring Central City, the town retained many of its historical structures even decades after it had experienced anything remotely similar to its boom days. Clearly, all of the action was in Central City.

Once a bustling building that housed a bar and crib rooms for prostitutes, Black Hawk's Toll Gate Saloon had fallen into disrepair by 1941 when this family of tourists posed in front of it. The saloon was on the first floor, while the crib rooms occupied the upper floors. The building eventually fell to the wrecking ball.

One of the few bright spots during Black Hawk's decline was the Black Forest Inn, opened by Bill and Kay Lorenz on Gregory Street in 1957. Nationally known for its German food, the restaurant was a frequent stop for operagoers and other people passing through town until it moved to nearby Nederland in 2000.

Another popular attraction in Black Hawk was the Lace House, first built in 1863 by Lucien Smith and remodeled in the 1880s by Samuel and Lydia Osborne. The Carpenter Gothic house became one of the most beloved landmarks in Colorado, appeared in several books, and became a popular tourist attraction after a 1976 restoration.

Other activities were soon incorporated into the busy summer season in Central City. The town's first Lou Bunch Day, held in honor of Central City's most infamous madam, was in 1974. The event, captured by photographer Dwayne Easterling for a postcard, included bed races on Main Street, a costume contest, and a ball. The event has consistently been voted one of the best mountain festivals in Colorado. (Courtesy of David Forsyth.)

From 1977 until 1992, the Central City Jazz Festival drew jazz bands from throughout the country to perform in the small mountain town. The groups played in several venues, including the Belvidere Theater, the Gilded Garter restaurant, and the Central City Opera House. This is a scene from the 1988 festival parade on Main Street.

While it appeared that Central City was thriving as tourism kept the town hopping in the 1950s, 1960s, and 1970s, there were signs that the century-old town was aging badly. The Knights of Pythias building, pictured here in 1960, was an extreme example of the decay starting to plague both towns. These problems ultimately led to the 1990 legalization of gambling in Black Hawk and Central City.

96

Five

FROM MINING GOLD TO MINING WALLETS
1990–2000

By the mid-1980s, it was clear that age was taking a toll on Black Hawk and Central City. Historical buildings, roads, and sewer systems were crumbling. The towns were simply falling apart, and no one had the money to make the necessary repairs. The population in both towns was dropping, which led to decreased tax revenues and worsened their financial problems. Tourists were also starting to look to other places in Colorado for recreation, especially ski areas, which were working to attract tourists in summer and fall instead of just winter. In Central City, a group of citizens formed Central City Preservation Incorporated and the Preservation Initiative Committee. Banding together with Black Hawk and Cripple Creek (about 140 miles to the south), they worked toward legalizing limited-stakes gaming in the three towns, with portions of the proceeds designated for statewide historic preservation efforts. On November 6, 1990, Colorado voters overwhelmingly passed Amendment 4 to the state constitution, and the three mountain towns soon buzzed with workers as construction transformed many of the historical buildings into casinos. Operators poured millions of dollars into the buildings; anywhere from $7,000,000 to $17,000,000 went into the stabilization and remodeling of the Teller House. The boom was back for Black Hawk and Central City, although Central City initially had far more business than Black Hawk. Gamblers would sometimes park a mile or more away and ride shuttles into town, where they would stand in line for hours outside of the crowded casinos waiting for the fire marshal to determine that enough people had left in order to allow more inside. Within a few years, however, the situation changed as newer and larger casinos opened in Black Hawk, which soon had the majority of gaming business in the state. Since the mid-1990s, the role of the two towns has been reversed, with Black Hawk the more popular and dominant of the two towns, but the rivalry that has always marked their existence remains alive and well.

The intersection of Highway 119 and Gregory Street in Black Hawk in the 1980s was about as quiet as the same area had been for the past 30 years or more. The one gas station that served Black Hawk and Central City by this time was just to the right of the Black Hawk Grocery Store on Highway 119.

Buildings in the two towns continued to deteriorate, sometimes due to age and at other times to more extreme causes, such as the fire that caused serious damage to the Gilpin Hotel in the late 1980s. Repairing the damaged buildings was becoming increasingly problematic for the cash-strapped towns that had once wielded such enormous economic power in Colorado.

Outside of the Memorial Day–to–Labor Day tourist season that packed the town, Central City was just as quiet as Black Hawk. Looking west at Main and Eureka Streets in this late-1980s photograph, very few tourists are on the streets. The Teller House, however, continued to dominate the view of the town, as it had done for more than a century.

Looking north at Central City from the Glory Hole tailings piles (which had been turned into parking lots for the thousands of tourists that visited the town), this image shows a slightly more active scene, with several cars parked in a lot at the end of Main Street on the lower right. The decrease in activity, however, remained worrisome to town leaders.

This overview of Main Street from the 1980s, with the Glory Hole Tavern in the lower left corner, shows no one on the streets of Central City. The deterioration of the buildings is also evident, demonstrated by the crumbling Ancient Order of United Workmen (AOUW) sign on the Glory Hole. Builders would soon find that the foundations of the some of these buildings had rotted away, leaving the buildings essentially floating.

Snow covers the hills behind the Glory Hole Tavern and Gilded Garter, two of the most popular places in Central City during the summer, on a very quiet and cold winter day. Black Hawk and Central City leaders wanted an activity that would draw people, even on days like this, while providing money to fix and maintain the aging towns.

For years, people argued that gambling would solve the towns' financial problems and that the territorial charters allowed it. Testing the theory in 1964 by taking part in a staged dice game are, from left to right, Gilpin County sheriff Vern Terpening, Deputy Sheriff C. Frank Bazzell, Monty Salisbury, and Bob Okey. The Colorado Supreme Court eventually ruled that statehood had voided the charters. (Courtesy of David Forsyth.)

In 1990, business and political leaders in Black Hawk, Central City, and Cripple Creek worked to get Amendment 4 to the Colorado State Constitution, which would legalize casino gambling, on the ballot. A key part of the argument that persuaded voters to approve the measure was that a percentage of the proceeds that would go toward statewide historic preservation projects.

As soon as voters approved Amendment 4, property values within the gaming districts in Black Hawk and Central City skyrocketed, and nearly every building and available lot in both towns went up for sale. The days of the businesses that had characterized Central City's Main Street since the 1930s, such as museums and rock shops, were numbered.

Crews quickly went to work transforming the former mining towns into casino towns. In this photograph from August 1991, a construction crew passes in front of what would become Annie Oakley's Casino between the Belvidere Theater and the Glory Hole Tavern (itself on its way to becoming a Harrah's Casino). Many of the buildings were in such poor shape that they had to be gutted. (Courtesy of David Forsyth.)

This image of the stabilization work on the Glory Hole demonstrates how badly deteriorated the buildings were. Construction crews faced numerous challenges; not only did they have to preserve the historical exteriors of Central City's buildings, they also had to make them welcoming spaces for gamblers. In many cases, holes were cut through walls in order to convert neighboring buildings into one large casino.

In order to remind visitors of how badly the town had deteriorated, some architectural damage was left in place, such as the very visible dip in the front of the Gold Coin Casino (renamed Easy Street in 2000) on Main Street. The Glory Hole's crooked door frame was also left as an example of the desperate situation that existed before legalized gambling arrived.

Despite vocal critics and unintended consequences, the massive restoration project did give many of the buildings in Central City a new lease on life, and although the Toll Gate did not last for long as a casino, the fact remained that the structure that housed it was still standing almost 12 decades after it was built.

In the rare cases where new construction was allowed in Central City, the design had to match the Victorian-era appearance guidelines that Central City's Historic Preservation Commission put in place. One of the few new buildings, the short-lived Bullwhacker's Casino on Main Street, appeared to be five historical buildings from outside but was, in fact, one new building.

More common was a mix of old and new construction, as seen in the Central Palace Casino. The 1863 Raynold's Court building is on the left, while the new part of the casino is on the right. This preserved the historical building while giving the bustling casinos the space they needed for their customers.

Harvey's Wagon Wheel Casino (renamed Reserve Casino in 2011), the largest casino in Central City, did incorporate and preserve two historical buildings: the small house on the left side of the casino and the tower visible above the Harvey's sign by the train, which was part of Central City's original electric system. Engine No. 71, no longer in use as a tourist attraction, also found a new home at Harvey's.

On October 27, 1991, people lined up to get into the Teller House for the first day of gambling. The line formed because the crowds were so big that the fire marshal refused to allow any more people inside the building until others left. Although two casinos have gone bankrupt in the Teller House, it still holds Colorado Gaming License No. 1.

Rows of slot machines occupy what was once the lobby and dining room area in the Teller House hotel. The original check-in desk, which would have been just past the lower right corner of the picture, was put into storage along with the rest of the original furniture from the hotel.

People had fun playing poker and blackjack inside the Teller House. These were the only two table games allowed in the gambling towns until statewide approval in 2008 and local approval in 2009 changed the rules, allowing craps and roulette and also raising the betting limit from $5 to $100. Under the new rules, casinos could also be open 24 hours a day as opposed to closing at 2:00 a.m.

With thousands of new visitors descending on Central City, casinos established a shuttle system to bring people from faraway parking lots to the heart of town. Some of the parking lots that people had to use were nearly a mile away, and parking within the city was at more of a premium than it had ever been.

The casinos were so popular that they quickly forced out the restaurants, souvenir shops, and similar businesses that had once drawn people to Central City. While that was not the intention of those who had pushed for legalized gambling, they could not deny that the casinos did pack the streets of Central City with new visitors. The casinos also brought fast-food restaurants to Gilpin County for the first time ever, including a McDonald's, Taco Bell, and Burger King. Out of all of the casinos seen in this picture, only Dostal Alley and the Bonanza remained in business by 2013. (Courtesy of David Forsyth.)

The Gold Mine Casino, located on Highway 119, was the first casino to open in Black Hawk. The town took a less restrictive approach to historic preservation than Central City, making it easier for new buildings to go up. The Gold Mine partially occupied the land where the gas station had once stood.

Rows of slot machines filled the Gold Mine Casino, which was much bigger than almost any of the casinos in Central City's historical buildings. Although it was initially quite popular, bigger and flashier neighboring casinos soon drew enough business away that it was forced to close, despite the fact that two other casinos within walking distance remained in business. (Courtesy of David Forsyth.)

Each new casino in Black Hawk seemed to be bigger than the last one. The Lodge Casino, seen here under construction in 1999, was one of the biggest, but it would soon be overshadowed by an even bigger casino located across Highway 119 from it. The larger casinos of Black Hawk also frequently had free parking garages, giving the town an advantage over neighboring Central City.

This photograph looks over the Lodge Casino to the blast site for what would become the Black Hawk Casino by Hyatt in 2001 (later renamed the Ameristar Casino after its purchase by that corporation in 2004), the largest casino in Black Hawk. The building would eventually include a 33-story hotel and spa, finished in 2009, and would be visible from the Coeur d'Alene Mine above Central City.

The formerly quiet intersection of Highway 119 and Gregory Street in Black Hawk looked vastly different in 2000 than it had in the 1980s. The church and school still stood above the town, but they were now city hall and the police headquarters. Bullwhacker's Black Hawk casino is in the middle of the picture, and the Black Forest Inn is visible behind it.

Looking down the north side of Black Hawk's Main Street toward the Lodge Casino in this 2000 view, the Bull Durham Casino building was one of the few historical structures left on Main Street. One of the town's many parking garages is visible between Bull Durham and the Lodge. One consequence of the larger casinos and parking garages was that relatively few people ever made it to the streets to walk around.

Looking east down Black Hawk's Main Street in 2000 gives a better view of the Lodge Casino and the Mardi Gras Casino just beyond it. Fitzgerald's Casino, seen on the right, occupied a mix of new and historical buildings and even fully encased one historical structure, Ben Olson's former sweet shop.

Looking west on Black Hawk's Main Street toward Gregory Street in 2000 provides another dramatic view of the changes gambling brought. The once-lonely Gilpin Hotel is fully surrounded by new structures, and the three buildings beyond it are also new construction; the fourth is one of the historical parts of Fitzgerald's Casino.

Historic buildings converted to casinos line Gregory Street in Black Hawk in 2000 at about the point where the Colorado Central Railroad trestle used to cross over the street. The Black Forest Inn is on the left side of the street, visible just above where the cars are. The large brick building on the west side of it is an addition put on when it became a casino.

The City of Black Hawk moved several historical homes into the Mountain City Historic Village, located on the western end of the town, to serve as city offices. Meant to recall the long-gone mining community of Mountain City, it was also a place to preserve some of Black Hawk's historical buildings. The city eventually moved the Lace House to this complex in 2008.

After several years of declining gaming revenue, Central City attempted to revive its economy with a new road into town from Interstate 70 and a large parking garage on the east end of town, but the majority of gamblers had long since moved to Black Hawk and its larger, more modern casinos. In a stunning reversal, Black Hawk was the thriving town while once-dominant Central City tried to catch up.

In 2000, less than 10 years after legalized gambling arrived in Gilpin County, Central City's Main Street was nowhere near the jam-packed thoroughfare it had once been. While the casinos persevered, summer activities like the Central City Opera and the Gilpin County Arts Association saw their importance increase as they were once again responsible for drawing large numbers of tourists to the town.

Six

THE LITTLE KINGDOM OF GILPIN
1859–2000

Although Gilpin County was the smallest county in Colorado for years, its political and economic power were undeniable and led many to refer to it as "the Little Kingdom of Gilpin." Black Hawk and Central City were the two best known of Gilpin County's many towns, but they were not alone. American City, Nevadaville, Pinecliffe, Deadwood Diggings, Gilpin, Gold Dirt, Kingston, Missouri Flats, Springfield, Nugget, and Vermillion were the names of just a few of the towns and camps scattered throughout the county. Nearly all were centered on mining operations, and some lasted only a matter of weeks or months before being abandoned or absorbed into larger towns. Dog Town, for example, was between Central City and Nevadaville. So named because of the large number of dogs that reportedly lived there, it disappeared, becoming part of Central City once that town was incorporated. Others were thriving cities in their own right at one time, with baseball teams, schools, and bustling Main Streets. Nevadaville, little more than a ghost town in modern times, once had a population of over 800 and was home to 13 saloons. Rollinsville, founded by John Quincy Adams Rollins in 1859, was unusual in that it did not allow saloons, dance halls, or gambling within the city limits. Tolland was also dry, a clause in each property deed stating that no liquor could be sold within its borders. Some of these towns survive today, but with nowhere near the population of which they once boasted. Others, however, are no more than dim memories, recorded in old deeds, newspaper articles, and photographs. The images that follow tell the story of a few of these once thriving places.

Originally named Nevada City after a California town, the city became Nevadaville when the US Post Office Department insisted on a different name. Leadville's mining boom in the 1870s cut its population in half. William Muchow's Glory Hole brought about a small revival, but after World War II, Nevadaville's population went into an irreversible decline. This is the business part of town in the 1880s; Main Street is in the lower-right corner.

In addition to its own school, Nevadaville also had its own Methodist church, the white building with the attached steeple seen in the lower left corner of this photograph. This was the residential section of Nevadaville, but mining dominated even there, as seen by the number of mine structures close to the houses. Almost none of these buildings survive today.

This photograph looks south from the residential section of Nevadaville toward the California Mine, which, at over 3,000 feet, was the deepest mine in Gilpin County. Today, the ruins of these mines still dot the hills around what is left of Nevadaville, which is little more than a ghost town itself.

Nevadaville also boasted its own school, though it was not as large as those in some of the other communities. The entire school poses for their picture in this photograph from about 1910. By the 1920s, the population had grown small enough that Nevadaville's students were served by the schools in Central City.

American City, west of Apex in the Pine Creek Mining District, was founded by US Navy and Civil War veteran Capt. Edward Marshall Stedman in 1899. Stedman owned the Mascot Mine, seen here, around which the small town was based. The mine produced enough ore that backers felt justified in building the Boston & Occidental Mill in order to process it on site.

In this American City view, James Peak is in the distance, while the building known as Snug Harbor is to the right. Although the town was short-lived, it was the setting for several Western movies made by the Selig-Polyscope Picture Company of Chicago in 1911. Two—*Why the Sheriff Is a Bachelor* and *Western Hearts*—starred Tom Mix.

In addition to the mine and mill, American City boasted several other buildings that were surprising for such a small town, including a school, which also served the nearby town of Nugget once its own school closed; the Hotel Del Monte, a popular stop for tourists; and Snug Harbor, seen in this picture. The original use of the building remains a mystery.

One writer referred to American City as being among the most picturesque and best preserved of all the ghost towns in Colorado, in part because of its unique architecture. The Castle, seen here in 1899, was one of the buildings that prompted that description. Unfortunately, a fire destroyed the structure in August 1990.

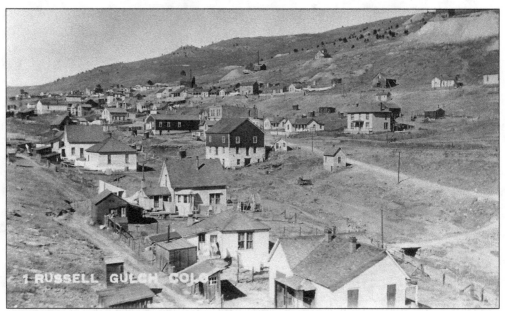

William Green Russell discovered gold in Russell Gulch shortly after John Gregory made his discovery on May 6, 1859. By the end of that summer, nearly 1,000 people had moved in, but that number dropped to 600 by October 1860. Over the next 20 years, the population steadily fell, though a few families still call the spot home today. Russell Gulch was a popular area for bootleggers during Prohibition.

The residents of Russell Gulch built a large brick school for the town's children. Its size almost rivaled that of neighboring Central City's large stone school, and though it is no longer in use, it still stands today. In this picture, the members of the fourth-grade class for the 1909–1910 school year pose outside the building.

Like people in many other towns in Gilpin County, Russell Gulch's residents enjoyed baseball, and the town had its own team that traveled around the county and state for games. In this picture from 1910, a game is in progress at Russell Gulch's baseball field, which, although not as elaborate as Central City's, still drew a sizable crowd for what was then a very small town.

A crowd gathers to watch what is possibly a horse race in the business district of Apex in 1898. The town, seven miles northwest of Central City, was founded in 1895; before the end of that year, there were nearly 100 houses there and over 800 the following year. Apex also boasted three hotels, a dance hall, and several saloons and was a popular destination for early tourists.

Despite its abundance of saloons, churches and schools were also an important part of life in Apex, as they were in most of Gilpin County's towns. Residents are heading to church on a Sunday morning in this picture from the early 1900s. Apex's school is visible through the trees just beyond the church.

A fire in 1939 destroyed most of Apex's business district, seen here in 1943. The town remained a popular location for summer homes, however, and was also the site of Gilpin County's only ski slope, the Apex Ski Area. Founded by World War II veterans, it had two tow ropes that pulled skiers to the top of the run. It was short-lived, operating from 1947 until the early 1950s.

Trains remained an important part of Gilpin County's life in the 1920s. Railroad owner David Moffat had dreamed of a tunnel through the Continental Divide before his death in 1911, but construction did not start until 1923. The town of East Portal sprang up to provide housing for 500 men hired to do the job. A railroad station, school, post office, and medical clinic were among the buildings.

East Portal remained an active community into the 1940s. During World War II, guards were posted on the Moffat Tunnel entrance 24 hours a day to protect against sabotage. By the 1950s, however, new technology along the railroad made it unnecessary to keep employees in the town, and only a few maintenance workers remained in the once bustling community.

Tolland began in 1893 when Charles H. Toll bought 956 acres in South Boulder Park to build a reservoir for land he owned near Broomfield. After his death, his wife, Katherine, renamed the area that had been known as Mammoth to Tolland and opened a hotel. Like Apex, Tolland was a popular tourist destination served by excursion trains from Denver. Property deeds explicitly banned the sale of liquor in the town.

The Tolland Hotel and the town's pool hall were the last surviving businesses in 1949; all other buildings were boarded up. In 1955, someone mistakenly threw hot ashes inside an icehouse filled with sawdust, creating a raging fire that destroyed the hotel and its outbuildings. The town was left nearly vacant with the exception of a few summer cottages.

As important as trains were to Tolland, its first train depot was actually a converted boxcar. The Denver, Northwestern & Pacific Railroad Company dismantled this Denver depot and moved it to Tolland, giving the town a real train station. The depot is seen here in 1972, long after it had seen its last train arrive. The path visible in the mountain behind it is known as the Giant's Ladder.

Trains passing over the Continental Divide were a frequent sight in Tolland as they moved passengers and freight around the country. No matter the time of year, the puffs of smoke from their smokestacks were a constant. In winters, snow sometimes piled along the tracks as high as the trains themselves, but the smoke still rose above them.

Prospectors found gold in the area of Baltimore in the 1880s, and the town boomed. Many hoped it would become a railroad town with construction of a line in South Boulder Valley, but it never happened. John and Lillian Hatfield kept the town alive with an opera house and social club (the ruins of which are pictured), but after their deaths in the 1930s, the town slowly disappeared.

The liquor-free town of Rollinsville is seen in this photograph from 1926. While town founder John Quincy Adams Rollins did not allow liquor, gambling, or dance halls, he did build a hotel, assay office, and stamp mill and owned over 400 mining claims. His Toll Gate Barn, which was used for his wagon road, still stands and is known as the Stage Stop Inn.

Lincoln Hills was the only black vacation resort west of the Mississippi River when it opened in 1922. Wink's Lodge, built by Obrey "Wink" and Naomi Hamlet, opened in 1928 as the first full-service resort in Lincoln Hills. It became a popular escape for musicians performing in Denver's Five Points neighborhood jazz clubs, including Lena Horne, Count Basie, and Duke Ellington; it was named a National Historic Landmark in 1980.

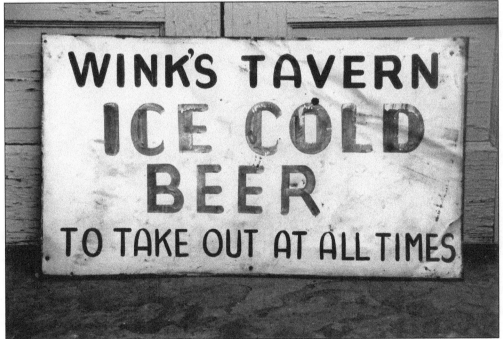

In addition to owning the Lodge, Wink Hamlet was also responsible for law and order in Lincoln Hills. Not only was he the game warden and fire lookout, but the county sheriff also deputized him to enforce the law. The tavern is one of several original buildings remaining in Lincoln Hills and has changed hands only a couple of times since Wink died in 1965.

Visit us at
arcadiapublishing.com

Printed in the USA
CPSIA information can be obtained
at www.ICGtesting.com
LVHW081652091123
763115LV00084B/634